SARDINES IN MY
SADDLEBAGS

From Florida to Alaska, In Between and Home

JOE T.

BALBOA.
PRESS

A DIVISION OF HAY HOUSE

Balboa Press books may be ordered through booksellers or by contacting:

Balboa Press
A Division of Hay House
1663 Liberty Drive
Bloomington, IN 47403
www.balboapress.com
1 (877) 407-4847

Print information available on the last page.

ISBN: 978-1-5043-9423-9 (sc)
ISBN: 978-1-5043-9424-6 (e)

Balboa Press rev. date: 01/13/2018

6/10/17

Hello Cheryl <3

DENALI OR BUST!

Been riding hard, so just getting around to this journal. Left 6/4/17, Sunday and rode through 3 days of rain. Then it broke out beautiful, so here we are at Osage Indian Reservation in Oklahoma.

It's a great nowhere campground state park. Nice river with small falls and pools of water and rope swing. Jumped and swam a lot, smashing my head into bottom rocks trying to get 30 feet down where everyone said the bottom was, but I crashed into it at 12 feet.

First night stop was Opp, Alabama. Rode about 400 + miles in plenty of rain. Awesome campground on excellent lake full of fish. Swamped that first night by torrential downpour.

Next night made it to Natchez, Mississippi, then crossed bridge and stayed at campground on other side of the river in Vidalia, Louisanna. More rain riding about 340 miles. Much more rain. Then went to Lake Ouichter in Arkansas. Big rain most way and out ran what appeared to be monster storm wanting to be a tornado off our left side for near 50 – 60 miles in diameter. When we safely made it past the storm I began to sing "Break on Through To The Other Side" – Old Jim Morrison song.

It really looked as though we were riding underneath a developing tornado. Swam in Lake Ouichta, a big lake and walked. Nice scenery. The roads have been exceptionally fun and scenic. Rolling hills, roads with lots of curves and some of the best riding roads in America, according to Jay. Jay's birthday is Tuesday 13th June and he will be 65. His wife Patty on her own bike is Cheryl's age or so and I'm the youngest at 30 x 2. Half full! So averaging 300 miles a day and first day over 400 miles.

Next day went to Jay's niece and 81 year old brother in law's house in Arkansas on boarder of Missouri. We actually went in and out of Arkansas and Missouri 4 to 5 times in the same day to get to their home. Left the next day and made it to here at Osage State Park Indian Reservation, I mentioned starting this journal.

6/11/17

Wind picked up steadily through night and next day. We rode through America's "Dust Bowl" Oklahoma and into Kansas, the notorious outlaw land in cowboy days. The ride to me was worse than the rain because the wind and gusts most likely exceeded 50 knots, blowing me all over the road. Had to constantly lean into the wind and once was blown completely out of my lane into the next. Fortunately the traffic is sparse and no one occupied that spot. Just miles of endless farms from horse, cattle, hay, etc., and nothing else. Also, the heat was over 100 degrees F most of the day making it harder. However, the good news was we found a really nice new 2 room separate bedroom cabin with full kitchen, tv, bath, a/c for only $50, which we split. Good thing because the wind was too much for tents and would have blown away, especially since there were no trees to secure them. We're averaging 300 miles a day, but Patty felt we needed to push harder for time, though Jay and I felt we were doing fine as we estimate 12, 000 miles for whole trip. We've now covered 1,800 miles in 6 days. We have 9 weeks for this trip so the math says at 300 miles a day we should have 3 weeks to goof off, explore, etc. Today we're off to Pueblo, Colorado or thereabouts. Wind still blowing hard outside.

6/11/17

Here's where I part company with Jay and Patty. They argued a lot over nothing, maily Patty's obsessive need to leave early each day and routes to take, etc. To much stress, two is company and three is a crowd! I let them take a north route that we planned at the cabin and I then continued west, waving to them as I went by, surely pissing them off as I didn't tell them. However, I made up my mind that if they continued to act like they were in a race for time, mainly Patty who clearly had a bug up her ass, then I'd continue on my own. As the lyrics go in Marshall Tucker's song, "It won't be the first time this old cowboy spent the night alone", and I love it!

So I drove on to Royal Gorge, Colorado, an hour or two west of Pueblo, riding 330 miles. Took pictures of tallest suspension bridge in N. America surrounded by snowcapped Rockies. Camped for free, $2 to swim and bath at the KOA nearby. Departing soon to Steamboat springs, Colorado, crossing a 14,000 ft plus mountain range. No doubt, I'll be stopping to put on thermals and leather. A local cautioned me about the ice and snow up there and said they're still in winter conditions high up in Rockies.

6/12/17

Rode on past Steam Boat Springs, Co., approximately 315 miles today. Weather was nice, no snow or ice on passes through Rockies, but wind gusts 50 + knots made it hard to keep bike on road. Rode over elevations exceeding 10,000 ft with mountain tops + 14,000 ft. Spent several hours last night charting my course to Denali, Alaska. Will head up tomorrow toward Grand Teton, Wyoming, thence toward Missoula, Montana to see Lloyd and Deanna.

6/13/17

Jay's birthday (65th) – must have put a curse on me! I lost my passport somewhere in the middle of nowhere, Colorado. I think it dropped out of my handlebar bag when I took my sunglasses out. I stopped to take a picture of helicopters swooping low to snatch water from a pond to fight fires. I went on 90 miles to Vernal, Co., before I realized it was gone, so I went all the way back, searched for hours along desolate highway to no avail. Set up camp north of Vernal in scenic state park in Utah. Gun jammed and now useless. Rode approximately 350 – 400 miles, but only 100 miles north of last place.

6/14/17

Wow! You should see me now! Camping in a wilderness site surrounded by snow and the majestic Teton mountains in Wyoming. What a difference a day can make. Woke up bummed out about loosing my passport and thinking Ive just "bust" Denali, but dear Cheryl worked hard to keep me going and Alaska is back on. Found out I only need my birth certificate and driver's license and the Canadian Authorities will let me through. ☺ So today I rode 265 miles though some of the most amazing and scenic land America has. Just incredible mountains on the high plains all snow capped with views of 100 + miles in any direction with only a few scattered cars/trucks. I'm writing this in bear country with my shotgun beside me. This camp is 10 miles down a 4 WD dirt road full of pot holes and washouts. The local warden told me today is the 1ˢᵗ good day in a while as it's been rainy, windy and cold. Still cold, dropping into low 40s with snow beside my tent. No one hardly is here but a few people and a bear was spotted today. Also, it's now close to dark, so I've locked my food up in bear storage bins and looking for elk, bear and deer in surrounding camp site. Ice cold stream running beside campsite. Totally awesome! Also unjammed my shotgun after setting up camp and feel much safer. This is true wilderness in the lower 48 states. So dear Cheryl & kids, I now celebrate you all and LIFE with a bottle of Grand Marnier (Airline size) I saved just for this occasion in paradise. Miss you all, but never felt so free out here on my own. Love & kisses your way! <3

6/15/17

Departed the wilderness camp in Tetons. Takes one hour to drive bike out 10 miles on rugged dirt road. Had to stop and stretch before cruising on hard top. Swam in Granite Hot Springs and bathed in 85 – 90 degree F water surrounded by snow capped Tetons. Mind blowing beauty on earth. Rode 250 miles through Wyoming. Now in Idaho riding the Sawtooth mountain range, elevations 12,000+ ft. Camped beside lake in Maccay, Idaho surrounded by highest snow capped mountains in Idaho. Once again, spectacular scenery and I still am the only tent camper with or without a bike. Good nite paradise.

6/16/17

Rode 350 miles today to Flathead Lake, north of Missoula, Mt., 20 miles or so south of Kallispell at Glacier National Park. Ride today was cold and wet, but I was warm enough and completely dry in all my gear, including full leather jacket, vest and chaps with rain gear over them. Staying at Lloyd and Deanna's on lake. Beautiful home in beautiful land. Appears I may not be able to get to Alaska due to passport problems, as the American side is a royal pain in the ass. I'll ride to the border tomorrow, about 1 ½ hours ride north of here to see what I can do, if anything at all.

6/17/17

Felt like I was in Sandals resort…which I've never been to, but couldn't be much better than Lloyd and Deanna's magnificent lake front home on Flat Head lake in Montana. They've been great hosts taking me out to dinners and showing me around. Everything is good and back on again… Denali, here I come. Rode to Canadian Border today. Trial run of 110 miles each way to find out my paperwork's in order and now all set to leave in morning on Father's Day 2017. It appears I've actually got nearly 2,000 miles to ride in Canada before entering Alaska. May take up to one week in Canada each way. Plan to stay in Banff National Park first night.

6/18/17

Father's Day and I'm 200 miles north of Canadian border and on my way. Made another 300 miles today even though my leisurely departure time of 1pm from Lloyd and Deanna's. Scenery beautiful all the way, snow capped mountains. I'm in a nice camp ground with all facilities. Leave tomorrow earlier hopefully to new amended route toward Banff National Park up Hwy 93 through Canadian Rockies. Will be colder, but more scenic than route previously planned. Hope to make it to Sugar Bowl Grizzly Den Provincial Park not far from Prince George and ½ way up Alaskan highway.

6/19/17

WIPEOUT!

I survived! Thanks no doubt to my ole departed buddy and my guardian angel, Bruce Shultz. This ride to Alaska I'm doing in honor of him and I've even nicknamed my Harley, Bruce. I've known him since we were in diapers and until he passed away on 3/17/12, St. Patricks Day, at the age of 54. He was said to be the longest continuous dialysis patient in America if not the world. For over 40 years, he never got off dialysis, but he was my inspiration and hero and sometimes pain in the ass because he always tried to analyze me and be my "shrink"! So today I ran off the highway going around a curve at least 60 MPH and the shoulder dropped off over a foot. So I then proceeded to drive this 800 lb machine like a dirt bike down a gravel embankment that sloped downhill a long way, until I no longer could and then crashed. The windshield flew off as well as all my camping gear, other pieces and me. I was unscathed and fortunately other drivers behind, saw and stopped to help me put my bike back together and drag it uphill with me powering the Harley for 50 to 100 yards until we got it back up to the road again. After straightening the crash bar and foot pegs and minus quite a few scratches on the tank and fender, "Bruce" was ready for more adventure. The two guys who helped me said they saw the whole thing and thought I was a "gonna" or as the one guy said it was a "shitty" wreck. I was heavily padded with my leather gear due to the cold and Travis helped me save my head with that excellent helmet he bought me for $500. I wiped out right abeam the Columbia Ice Fields in Alberta, Canada and either a gust of wind hit me or I lost concentration around the curve, or both. Anway, I continued on another 150 to 200 iles and I'm now back in British Columbia and about 1 ½ hours form the Alaskan Highway which I will be on for another 1000 – 1500 miles before I get to Alaska. Stopped along the way and got some nice pictures of a big black bear alongside the road. I'm now in Pacific mountain time for the next month or more. I'm tired and sore and ready to sleep. Good nite! Really miss my wife and kids.

6/20/17

Today felt incredible. Epic! I've been smiling all day inspite of the first 100 miles riding in cold rain. I was completely warm and dry except my hands which got wet and froze. Went through 3 pairs of gloves. Wow! What a day. Rode close to 400 miles, got in at 11pm with fading light to set up camp on Moberly Lake, ½ hour or so south of Dawson Creek. Truly wild and free and scary out here alone. Came across 3 bears today. A big brown hangin out with a black bear next to the road. Just me and them. I stopped just past them 30 – 40 yards, but kept engine running as they looked like they liked me, but ambled off. Then 10 – 15 minutes later I stopped by a black bear on side of road then I done something really stupid, I didn't want to spook the bear so I cut my engine off before I got to him and coasted in close. The bear went up to the woods only feet away and I realized my bike wouldn't start. Took too long and that could have been a bad mistake. Must stop pressing the envelope. Rick, a real mountain critter lives down the road, drives his own logging truck, tells me the black bears are more dangerous because they're curious with hunger on their minds. He said he sometimes has up to a dozen grizzlys on his property regularly, but they tend to move on when they see people unless they don't want to. He said there's been quite a few fatalities here last year or so, some eaten and always black bears. I believe the brown bear I saw with the black was probably a black with a brown coat as opposed to a grizzly with also have been known…..I think to hang out with the black. Anyway, totally awesome. Keep my shotgun next to me in camp ready to defend myself "if" I get ½ a warning. Rick noticed my back tire is looking bald. Well, I'd been thinking about it most of the day knowing a flat out here, I'd be shit out of luck. He verified it and said I'm coming up on Fort St. John and an hour or so over next mountain a bigger town – might find Harley shop. Also stopped off in Prince George, British Columbia a coupla hours back and found cannabis dispensary which gave me a yearly card. Fantastic! Truly Rocky Mountain High! It's 2am, good nite!

6/21/17

Hello Summer and longest day of the year. Good thing as I had another long day getting in camp by 10pm with light to 11pm. They say "discretion is the better part of valor" so I decided to err on the side of caution and turn back down hwy 97 from near Dawson Creek to Prince George again, another 3 hour back track. Turns out I needed to replace the rear tire as there's no place that can happen for next 1000 – 1500 miles of Yukon wilderness. So back again I go and get oil change as well as new tire. Once again, saw 2 more bears in "Pass" as they call it here, a passage across mountain range and full of wildlife. The pass (stretch) is between McBride, BC and Chetwynd, BC, about 60 – 100 miles. Today one bear was huge! At least 800 or 1000 lbs. Maybe grizzly, but I think big black. I stopped abeam him, still good ways, away, 75 – 100 yards, but he looked very intimidating. Looked at me several times and walked on slowly looking back. A couple Canadian guys on Harleys helped me out and we all were heading back to Prince George which they recommended I do. They saw a moose on same stretch I saw bear. Awesome? Right now I'm probably foolishly eating as I write in my tent past midnight, but I have munchies! Especially since not only am I the only tent camper anywhere. Most all have trucks with campers, but I set up away from everyone about 100 yards out in middle of field next to lake. Little spooky, but all in the sport of it! I haven't seen a tent camp in over a week. Happy Birthday, Coco Puff, Love you and everyone.

P.s. going to stash my munchies on my Harley parked 30 feet away. "night".

16

6/22/17

Coco's 29 today

My baby has her own baby, Everett Joseph Wynn, who's rapidly approaching 2 months. I toast you all on your birthday from Clements Lake, in Stewart, BC. Cheers! This camp is everybit as spectacular and scary as the Teton wilderness Camp. Alaska is less than one mile away, except I detoured unexpectantly as I made the wrong turn out of Meziadin Lake Park, which I decided not to stay due to too many RVs and truck campers. Anyways, I went another 80 to 100 miles out of my way as I inadvertently took alternate 37A off the Alaskan Hwy 37. I ended up in the last town here in BC, called Stewart. A really cool family with dad told me about this camp site which I actually turned into before I ran into them 5 miles or so from here, and had left because it was spooky. Bears everywhere. Only a few miles from here I stopped just past a mom black with her cub. I kept my engine running while stopped and snapped a picture. As soon as I did she turned right towards me, looked pissed, and in my haste to leave since she was only 30 yards from me, I ejected the batteries out of camera. Well this camp is free, right on Alpine Lake with snow capped mountains and meadows all around. Completely stunning beauty, but dangerous for dummies like me tent camping as I'm the only one minus the tent beside me which appears the campers retreated to their car or truck. Only a couple people here. I feel like the other nut case who didn't fare well with his buddy bears out here. Anyway, for sure risky, as everyone says this place is loaded with black and grizzly. I've got my gun loaded in bag with me. This place is so remote, no one on highway for 60 miles or more, except me. Did run across one Canadian onhis Harley which was a Heritage like mine. I checked on him as he was stopped in middle of nowhere. Out here if someone is broke down it's imperative you help. He actually saw me again in the other RV site and thanked me for stopping to check on him. He was ok and a local from Stewart which appears to have a population of 50 – 100 people. The road 37A – Alaskan Alternate is probably the most awesome, beautiful highway I've ever been on, and well worth the detour as long as I don't become dinner tonight. Newly paved and perfect for a Porsche or Ferrari as long as you don't get killed by game all around. Also met Rhonda here smoking a joint with her 2 black snauzer dogs. She never stopped talking a minute and I was afraid she was staying, but she left. She was really nice, artist, teacher, eccentric and a lot like Susan Muholland. She invited me to her house to stay, but I politely declined. Maybe if she didn't talk so much. Kidding! Even though I'm next door to Alaska, the journey is to Denali National Park, home to Mt. McKinnley, 20,000ft and the North Pole. Did about 350 – 400 miles today. Most beautiful warm day. Totally awesome for cruising. Love it! Will enjoy before weather turns south in a hurry around here. It's still light at midnight and now it's 130am or so and only now dark.

6/23/17

Good morning sunshine! Another beautiful today! Total paradise here….
on this sunny day in June. Didn't sleep well due to paranoia of bears here.
Turns out a young couple, Andre and his girl, Canadians told me to not
worry but get bear spray. Said my gun only marginally effective if bear is
about to have me for dinner. He said I need to alternate shells with slug
rounds. So Rhonda last night and Andre said while I'm here with Alaska
just a few miles away, I should go visit the Salmon River Glacier in Alaska
just across the way. They said nothing in Denali compares to it and so I'm
on my way to Alaska.

6/24/17

Hyder, Alaska

Another full day in paradise. I'm back at the same camp on lake surrounded by incredible beauty and bears and it's totally awesome. Met some really interesting and cool people today. Rode 15 minutes from camp through hip and quaint border town of Stewart, BC right into Hyder, Alaska. No border immigration on American side because the road you're on only goes to a magnificient ice glacier, Salmon River glacier which is back in BC. As the mountain you look at splits our two countries, so you ride into Alaska and BC on same rough gravel, dirt road 20 miles each way. Ate breakfast and dinner in town, both excellent. Dinner $8.95, breakfast more. The people I met were amazing. One young German couple have been cycling (pedal) around the world, have already been through Europe, Asia, Malaysia, China and I met them on the Glacier just coming from Anchorage, Denali to now in the camp on the lake I'm staying at. One Canadian guy I saw on the highway, 2 -3 days ago whom I talked to at a gas station 600 miles back I see again on the Glacier. Cool dude riding a BMW off road type from Nova Scotia to BC over 5000 miles each way and camping like me. Some people were amazed that I drove my Harley out to the glacier, each way 20 miles and sometimes steep gravel road full of bumps and pot holes which I had to run in 1st or 2nd gear only. There were some dirt bikes, mostly a few trucks. It took me an hour and a half each way, so I decided to stay back here in bear country again. Feels safer tonight as there's now 4 – 5 camps here and we had a great fire going and everyone telling stories of their adventures while having a few nice drinks. Plenty of "joe stories". It's again around 2am as it's only dark at midnight and it's still not very dark.

6/25/17

Cold rain came and was planning to stay another night and try to wait rain out, but got nice break at noon, enough time to get going. Drove through intermittent rain next 300 miles, but warm. Enjoyed ride despite weather. I'm at Deese Lake camp by river. Only tent camper, all woods and shot gun loaded at arms length. Seen no bears today but they're here. Took wrong turn in here and drove Harley up hills and steep drop dirt roads ½ mile only dirt bikes or 4 WD use. Made it! White Horse tomorrow.

6/26/17

Yukon Territory

Covered 250 – 300 miles despite another slow start, partly due to rain and part fatigue. Riding in rain is hard long distance even if warm. Here you must constantly scan sides of road for game. So I slept in until almost 10am. People ask me how much time I got for trip. I tell them "I got no schedule, I got no place to be and I got no time to get there in". It's truly an amazing experience. I feel like easy rider X10. If my kids could only see me now…never without a shirt anymore. Plenty cold! Last night slept with 2 long sleeves and heavy jacket on top of me inside a 20 F sleeping bag. In Yukon now, getting steep mountainous. I intercepted Alaskan Hwy 1 which is beginning of Yukon territory. White Horse tomorrow!

6/27/17

Nice Day, covered 450 miles as much as 1st day leaving home. Camped at Moose Lake campground some 200 miles north of White Horse, still in Yukon. Should be in Dawson in 1 hour tomorrow and Alaska border just past Dawson. Met a man from Kansas on BMW and also camping. I've only seen one or 2 other tent campers besides Patty and Jay. He said the "Top of the World Highway" is pretty rough, most all gravel for 50 – 60 miles. More dirt biking on my 800 lb machine. Still having fun and completely into routine of "roughing it". Must say though I'm pretty "whooped" and missing home. Honey, can you cook me a nice breakfast? This is typical routine: wear same clothes for a week, except change socks every 3 days. On most cold days I wear 2 thermal tops, leather vest and heavy, lined jacket and gortex rain jacket. 1 thermal pants, jeans, leather chaps, gortex rain pants and trusty Rocky waterproof snake boots. Dinner tonight was sardine sandwich, BBQ chips, 4 pieces raw broccoli with ranch dressing, peach and snack of nutmix. Saw good size black bear today and got couple pictures. Guy on BMW said he tried to take Hwy 11 – Dalton hwy to Artic Ocean but had to turn back due to big storm approaching.

6/28/17

Arrived in Dalton after several hours. Everything is further than you think. I nearly ran out of gas as did many travelers, both on bikes (mostly BMW) or cars. One man offered me gas which I happily took. Dalton is just a little historic town on river. Had nice salmon fish sandwich and fish soup with salmon and halibut. Treat! Easy day today – part rain, rest lovely. Camping on other side of river after crossing on ferry. It's 1 ½ to 2 hours to Alaskan border crossing Dalton Range on hwy called "Top of the World". Lot of gravel, slow going expected but super scenic. Still some 8 hours to Fairbanks.

6/29/17

Real Alaska

Wow again! What a crazy trip this is. Last night I stayed wisely at the only camp ground before Alaska border. Was going to carry on to border before I thought better of it and turned back to camp. Good thing because not only would I have not made it to border before they closed at 9pm, but I would have been in middle of nowhere. 50 miles in any direction, absolutely nothing. Camp was pretty cool. Old, eccentric, super talented man ran and built place with his ingenuity. Had Sauna rooms to bathe in, where you make your own fire to boil water on wood stove. Nice library room with sofas, games, etc. All heavy duty wood construction. Met a Canadian girl from Montreal named Lily. Very nice and a lot like Aneta from Chezk Republic, I met in St. Helena. Lily is a free spirit girl, turned 23 today. Going to college but hitchhiking to places like the artic circle in Inuk, BC. She wanted me to take her to Fairbanks, Alaska, but I declined as she needed to stay in Dawson one more day so she could get to computers for college classes in town. She set her tent up on the edge of a cliff overlooking the Klondike River we just crossed. The cliff dropped more than a hundred foot only feet from her tent. It was a good think I didn't take her as we would not have made it. The ride was grueling, over 120 miles of rocky, bumpy, dirt road full of gravel. It was really tough on the Harley and me. Several times I almost wiped out in 1st gear, so with her on back we for sure would have crashed. Plus mom would have been pissed! Anyway, that road aptly named the "top of the world" hwy was the most magnificent scenery of Vista's mountain ranges, where you see for probably 100 miles or more and you're on the very top of the mountain pass (Dalton Range) the whole 120 miles. The road is only open 4 months of the year as the river freezes in October and when the ferry stops, the road closes. I'm in Alaska now, only 2 hours south of Fairbanks and it's around midnight, but light as day. It's Alaskan time zone, so 4am back home. I stopped along highway and camped only couple miles from a moose. I took pictures of. Tomorrow I'll be able to see Denali, as they say you can see it from Anchorage on a clear day. The mountain is over 20,000 feet tall. Lots of grizzly, everyone says in this area and especially Denali. Good night! As I've now rode nearly 7000 miles since home and over 2,700 miles in Canada.

6/29 1/2/17

I think my dates have been off 1 day

No bust for me, for I am in Denali! Camped at packed National Park camp ground. Everyone only 15 – 20 feet from next camper. Myself, 2 guys and girl from Atlanta got last 2 spots in park. They are cool people and really nice. They ventured off on 30 mile hike today, actually 4 days hiking they say. This is way too touristy for me, but I couldn't resist the fact they have hot showers. Been couple days since last and after crossing that 120 mile dusty Dawson Range and sleeping in wilderness, the $15 is worth it. Rode another 300 miles today stopping in Fairbanks and got some awesome weed from the legal pot shops. This one was called Paco Loco or something like that. Completely legal in Alaska. Farout! Also ate at nice authentic Italian Restaurant and continued on to Denali. I haven't seen the "big one" because it's still some 70 miles into this big National Park. They only allow people bussed in on tours up near mountain. No other vehicles and for 50 bucks and 8 hour tour, you're in! I'll find a way cheaper to see Denali in all it's glory and hopefully on a clear day. Plan to camp in next wilderness camp free and closest I can find to Denali.

6/30/17

Denali sighted! Success at last!

It is an awe inspiring sight to see Denali and her 2 sister peaks in all their glory! Am so blessed to still have eyesight and witness such beauty. The mountains are behind the Alaskan mountain range and another range, but at 14,000, 17,000 and 20,000 they're towering on the landscape and all covered in snow. Wow! I'm seeing Denali my way, camping on a riverbed between 2 rivers that flow off Denali, ice cold and fast running, and all for free. Plus there's the coolest hip town you've ever seen only 2 minutes walk off the riverbed. Potshop next door, fine restaurants and bars playing blues and various bands. Neat shops. Very quaint and very small. So I'm at Talkeetna, Alaska, ½ way between Fairbanks and Anchorage. Locals along the way told me about this "out of the way" and super cool town of phenomenal beauty and that I could camp on this riverbed and on a "good" day which is said to happen only once a week at best, then you see Denali at it's best. Right they were. So this town is 15 miles off the main highway and dead ends on this riverbed. All wilderness adventures launch from this place. Lots of sea planes, water rafting, mountaineering, etc. Most people know about it who are adventurous or get lucky like me by looking for just such a place. Luck was with me as the day became beautiful, warm, sunny and clear. I was still gazing at the big ones well after midnight which was as light outside as normal evening hours anywhere south. I met a fun bunch of kids – 25 – 30 year olds camping and partying from Anchorage. Really nice! One guy, Logan invited me to stay anytime and as long as I like at their home. They talked me into walking a few minutes into town where we partied in a bar packed with people, dancing everywhere and having great fun. I had a blast and woke up with big hangover. Theirs were bigger and today the police kicked them off the riverbed beach because they were rowdy. They really liked me and were amazed I rode my Harley alone, camping to Alaska. They had all sorts of names for me and because they saw me after I took my bath in the ice cold river with "no shirt on" as the day was warm, they were also going on and on about my abs. Hey Abacrombie Joe", etc., you should be a model. They don't realize I haven't worked out since leaving home, but once or twice. They were really fun. People super nice all through Canada and Alaska thus far. Sky clouded overcast and rained today,but now it's stopped and clearing up. Time to step out of my tent and into paradise.

7/1/17

Hello July 1ˢᵗ in Talkeetna

What another great day and night here in Talkeetna! Been running into the nicest, coolest people everywhere. The town is simply awesome. I've apparently become somewhat popular up here as many have heard about my crazy adventure and all sorts of people know me and come up to me and say "Hey Joe", and invite me to go to their homes, such as in Anchorage and a couple camping next to me invited me to go fishing on their boat in Seward, which is a big fishing town on the Kenai Penninsular. Last night I was in the same rocking bar as the night before where a great Minnesota Bluegrass Band was playing and people coming up to meet me and buy me drinks. Then I ran into the same people from Atlanta, GA who I was camping beside a few days ago, north of here in Denali Natl Park. Dean, Phillip and Elissa, who seem to think the world of me. Dean told me that I'm the "coolest" person they ever met up here and so we had a great time partying, dancing and hanging out by a big campfire on the riverbed by my tent until after 5am. I'm only now getting up after 4pm. Due to rain in anchorage and the Kenai Penninsula, I've decided to stay here until Tuesday the 4ᵗʰ July, which is when the rain is expected to clear up. Absolutely could not be stranded in a better place and so I'm enjoying myself and adventures immensely. Time to get out of my sleeping bag and head up town, 5 min walk for food and entertainment.

Just returned and heard from lots of people talking about the mother grizzly and her cubs walking straight down mainstreet this morning. Last night I mistakenly felt that there was no need to load my shotgun, before I crashed out. It turns out this riverbed I'm camping on at end of mainstreet and surrounded by 2 rivers full of salmon, soon spawning, happens to be grizzly playground!

7/4/17

America's birthday of idealism, namely the constitution which ideals become more elusive with each Degeneration. It's the integrity or lack thereof, the people as a Government cannot succeed if you don't live by the former. So Happy Birthday, America and good luck! My glass is apparently ½ empty, ha!

I seem to have lost time again as I was "stranded in paradise" or pretty close in Talkeetna, Alaska. Spent 4 days idle, but having fun until the last day or so. The skies went overcast with rain and cold and my mood went south in a hurry. Felt really sad and I left as soon as the rain broke on 4th July. The whole town came out for a big parade and people everywhere as I was leaving, but I didn't feel better until I passed Anchorage on my way to Seward. Sun finally came out and I felt much better. Went to major fishing village, Seward on Alaskan Penninsula. Thousands of fishing boats in harbor, big salmon, halibut and other fish hanging by seafood shops and processing. Now I'm camped in middle of purple flowered meadow in the middle of snow covered mountains in the heart of grizzly territory (shotgun ready).

7/5/17

Awesome camp spot last night- didn't sleep restfully as I was all alone in bear country. Seen no bear though. Probably a good thing. I'm camped now in the end of the Kenai Penninsula Spur on Cook Inlet. Can't get no further this way without a boat or wings. Nice camp site here, not many campers and had to pay $15 I'd rather not. Had the best shower of trip at the Seward Marine Harbor Master's facilities in that great fishing village. Paid $2 and had awesome hot water pressure. Was cold last night and tonight too, so out came the thermals. Been nice sunny weather thus far on Pennisula, which is rare, so good thing I waited it out at Talkeetna.

7/6/17

(PawPaw) Papa's 90th Birthday today

Couldn't find a journal, so 3x5s will have to do. Everything from before White Horse in the Yukon is very expensive in these far off places. Bags of chips $6 - $7 for 12 oz. The fishing villages of Seward and Homer the same. More expensive to buy a fish dinner of same fish in these areas as Florida. Camped on Homer Spit last piece of land a highway can take you to on Kenai Peninsula. Totally amazing scenery with all the fishing vessels surrounded by snow mountains.

Camped next to me is Angela, a woman from Sydney, Australia who flew all the way to Anchorage and rented a car to drive to Homer, her whole purpose for trip. She's just hiking and shopping, no fishing which is why most people come here. It's the halibut capital of the world and lots of salmon, kings, silvers and arctic Char. The tides change rapidly here. When I came in it was high. This morning it's a couple miles out. Met Dave on a Honda from Georgia. Dropped his medicine bag. I found it and returned it to him.

7/7/17

Another awesome day inspite of being pulled over by 2 Alaskan State Troopers and ticketed $160....ouch! For passing on a double line, right in front of their faces. Didn't see them and they didn't buy the glaucoma story! I left Homer which like Talkeetna, I absolutely love. Also Seward, but Homer has Seward beat as a fishing village. These boats don't have to go out too far, my guess as these waters are loaded from all the huge fish catches I see.

Before I left Homer I spent a long afternoon there enjoying the super cool fishing village, restaurants and Salty Dawg Saloon. No drinks, just bought shirts for boys. Had drink there last night. It's just like the Iron Horse Saloon, except 10 X cooler. I was all dressed to ride with all my gear on including thermal and leather then decided I had to jump in the Alaskan Gulf Ocean at the very end point one can get in a vehicle of any sort except boat or plane in N. America.

The Homer Spit juts out further into the Alaskan Gulf than anywhere else. The waters are glacier runoffs with a bit of ocean mixed in. Will wake you up in a hurry. People must have thought I was crazy, but I told them this wild trip is and may as well prove it. It's really a spectacular place and I would love to go fishing both there and Seward, but for now I'll save it for another day. Rode on 250 – 300 miles and 50 – 100 north of Anchorage. Camped by river bed on Kings River. Nice spot, free.

7/8/17

Rode 250 miles or so in cold rain.

Another great day, laughing as I'm riding, waving at all the bikes (pedal) as a race of more than 100 are pounding away like me in the freezing cold rain, but really having a good time. I was/am completely prepared and stay perfectly warm, except my hands which are always cold. Rode over 100 miles in cold rain, temperature in 40s and also very foggy. Because there was little traffic, I kept going, but it is more dangerous driving. I am sure these people will have thought me completely nuts as I was having entirely too good of a time in generally miserable conditions. So now I pulled off the highway 20 miles or so from Valdez. Decided to come here afterall as everyone told me what a great place and cruise. Once again, they're completely right. Awesome Alaska! It was still raining as I arrived around 730 – 8pm That's real early for me as I usually don't get into camp until 10pm.

This camp site is also awesome. No charge as I found another great area by a fast running high glacier river. I'm on a gravel bed 8 – 10 ft higher than the river. No doubt bear country, so got everything just so, axe, knife and bear spray one side of me and shotgun other side. Ate my sardine sandwich further upstream and had to throw can in river, which I don't like but better that than bear enticement. Across the fast river are waterfalls pouring down from snow covered mountains. Awesome!

Haven't been into Valdez yet, but most people say the weather is clearing tomorrow and can't wait to check it out. Another fishing village sitting on

Prince William Sound. I believe it's Saturday and the rain has stopped, but sky still heavy with dark clouds. Looking forward to another nice hot shower at the Harbor Masters. Like in Seward it's open to public, cheap and great. Last Dip in Alaskan gulf was a little too chilly to scrub up good.

I've been on the "road" for over a month now, covering over 8,000 miles. I feel like I've challenged myself to be tough and handle whatever comes my way. Oftentime it's mind over matter and the ability to look at obstacles as just another challenge. I'm so glad I talked myself into this trip, but it ain't over yet. Might be 1/2 way. Lots more challenges and interesting life along the way, like Grant and Marie. They are from Colorado and took my picture for mom on river.

7/9/17

Mama Ting's BD tomorrow <3 57

Love you baby! Happy Birthday Tomorrow, 10th July, baby! <3<3<3 and what a day it is. Sunny and warm. People were right and so glad I detoured in the cold rain 100 miles to this awesome campsite, some 15 – 20 miles from Valdez. Now that I can really see the scenery, it's totally wild and beautiful. The river has been roaring all night, but I'm all alone and loving it! Wish all you were here though. Today, later I'll go to Valdez and get my hot shower. Working on 3 days since last, phew! Gone exploring.

Time to eat peanut butter and jam and bananas while clothes dry on rocks. Just returned from 4 – 5 mile hike down a maintained gravel road used for service of Alaska pipeline which Valdez is the last terminous and unfortunately the place of one of America's worst oil spill many years ago in this paradise. Fortunately they did an excellent job of cleaning up in spite of the countless wildlife lost. Kept mace and gun at the ready. Only short way from campsite across river I found a mud bank near river which was full of fresh bear tracks and claw raking. Saw a friendly big owl. Old fellow named Larry told me about a nice mountain trail to hike here.

Just returned from Valdez and a long needed shower at the Harbor Masters. Ran out of hot water on my $4 token, then it was icewater from knees down. Ate a nice blackened halibut sandwich and returned to same campsite on river. Not before I ventured off on what I thought was the trail "Old Larry" told me about. I climbed up this mountain trail that followed a waterfall up the mountain, but it dead ended at a very dense forest deadfall. Didn't see any bear, but they're definitely there. As I was riding away I saw the 1899 pack trail head some ¼ mile past where I thought it was. I hope to hike it tomorrow before leaving, if it's not raining. As soon as I set up camp it started raining with lots of mosquitos out now. Need another break in rain like today, and on a good ride should cross border back in BC tomorrow. Not if it's raining though. I could be stranded again. This time there's no town nearby. I'm out here on this riverbed all alone. It's not good to hike out here without anyone knowing, so now you know that's my plan!

7/10/17

HAPPY 57 <3 birthday, Cheryl! I LOVE YOU!

Rode hard today through cold rain, most entire way some 300 miles. I didn't want to leave Alaska this soon, but as I say "discretion is the better part of valor". I saw a break in the rain, just long enough for me to break camp and get going. I wanted very much to hike the 1899 gold rush pack trail, I missed yesterday, but I knew if I went I could be stranded many days waiting for a cold rain to subside. Also for sure it is risky hiking in rugged bear country and no one knowing where you are should something go "south".

I pressed on despite not wanting to. I can't get enough of Alaska. I wish I had lived there many years ago. I didn't even scratch the surface so to speak, but I'm so grateful to experience it the way I am, camping and living in the wild even if for such a short time. I now do know I have it in me to be as rugged as any Alaskan and I sometimes feel like I'm living the wrong era and should have lived here in the 1800s. I also know I haven't scratched the surface of real Alaskan hardship.

I spent most 2 weeks in Alaska and rode over 2,000 miles – I'm now camped at the only "civilized" campground for the next 100 miles or more. You can't believe how great a hot shower feels when you've been on a motorcycle in the cold rains for 7 – 8 hours. I paid $15 to camp here and I probably used that much in hot water. My clothes and leather was thoroughly soaked, but I was completely warm and actually loving it. I was being a bit naughty to the "fancy" bikers riding BMWs on/off road machines. At one point I had slowed down on rough gravel roads most suited for the BMWs and not my big Harley. About!/2 dozen of these guys came blowing by me on the gravel, so I waited for the gravel to end and then I set to bearing down on them and promptly blew by them, waving and yelling #1 Harley. It certainly pissed them off and they kept trying to pass me, but I wouldn't let them, as I was flooring it! Eventually, I let a couple go by cuz I felt sorry for the rookies.

I'm only a few miles back into the Canadian side again at a place called Beaver Creek. It is the most western settlement in Canada. Not much between here and White Horse, the Gold ruse "jump off town of the 1800s. It's about 450 miles or so from here. Get to do some laundry in the morning. Been wearing same thermals, shirt and jeans for a week now. The freshest thing on me was my socks and they were worn 3 days. Who needs bear repellent? It's after midnight here as I just got in around 1030 at night.

7/11/17

Now I should definitely be discouraged. I've been riding for 2 days straight through cold rain, but today was as bad as I have been in. Everything is soaked, even my waterproof snake boots, feet and hands freezing most of trip. I rode nearly 350 miles today, a little past White Horse as the 450 estimated yesterday was kilometers. It rained hard for at least 200 miles and as I'm writing this, frost is blowing from my breath in the tent. I'm camping on Marsh Lake in Yukon. Tried to start fire but everything's wet so I'm in my bag. I had to wait until noon just to get a break long enough for rain to stop, to hurry and break camp. Much harder when everything's wet. Did get my laundry done and packed in plastic bags. After about 100 miles or so toward White Horse, I stopped at a small gas station and restaurant and met 2 guys from Los Angeles on BMWs. They said they saw me a week ago at Homer after I had jumped into the Alaskan Gulf. We were all freezing, and in no hurry to get started again. Sure doesn't feel like middle of July.

Without a doubt this part of Alaska and Canada is tough going as the roads are full of pot holes, washouts and gravel for hundreds of miles. Very few people (nuts) like me would attempt this on a Harley. I've only seen less than 10 or so in all of Canada and Alaska, but hundreds of BMW off road/on road types. I'm still having fun, despite hardships and love the journey. At my age (60), alone, camping the whole way on a Harley puts me in a whole new category of "nuts". Add to that....no smart phone... no radio...no gps!

7/12/17

Reprieve from rain today!

Revived! One nice day today. Everything's dried out if only for the day. Tomorrow, more rain forcasted and as I'm writing this at 2am or so, I had to run out and stake the tent as the wind kicked up hard and earlier watched the clouds roll in black, but it was a sunny, beautiful day earlier. Rode 350 miles or so back the direction I came and pulled into a campground in BC on Boys Lake. Scenery absolutely breathtaking. Pure crystal clear, emerald green lake, full of trout surrounded by snow covered tall mountains. Camp ranger said they had snow yesterday and I can believe it as cold as I was. I jumped in the ice cold lake and took a bath, soap, shave, the works. Out in 2-3 minutes. Wow! Today again, just spectacular and goes a long way to make up for the tough days. Met more really cool people here, all riding dirt bikes on their adventures. One young couple, our kids ages rode their dirt bikes from Oregon and going to farthest north you can go in Alaska on road to Prudaoe Bay, which only dirt bikes are feasible unless you're totally crazy. Over 1000 miles of gravel!

Well, after that they are then riding to bottom of South America and maybe around world. Also met and partied with Aaron from NZ, who rode his KTM 500 dirt bike from bottom to top, south and north islands of NZ. Then rode from bottom of S. America to Prudaoe Bay, Alaska and now working way back south where I met him and another couple Sam and his girlfriend (I forget her name). All super interesting and nice. Aaron took my picture after jumping in Lake Boys BC and will send it to lover girl,

Mama Ting when he gets a signal. We are very remote here and it's simply grand. So Aaron and I are tent camping on the nicest ground I've been on anywhere yet. Lovely short green grass only feet from the magnificient lake, but who knows what tomorrow will bring? There's reported fires everywhere further south and east of BC. Some 200 separate fires and some main highways are closed. Will try to figure out way back tomorrow with any new info we get as it's about the only way back. However, if I have to delay here, it's a great place. This next 500 miles to Kitwanga, BC is just paradise. Just like Alaska. Love it!!!

7/13/17

Back to Stewart, BC/Hyder Alaska

Sure enough the rain came again but not nearly as bad as 2-3 days ago. Still cold and rained through most half of the approximate 400 miles I covered today. Now back to my very favorite campsite on Lake Clements in Stewart, BC, only few miles from Hyder, Alaska. I first arrived at on Coco's birthday, 3 weeks ago, and close to where Jay and Patty later camped at and never continued further north because of the rains. I'm the only tent camper here. There's 3 other vehicles camping nearby which although they're quiet, I'd rather be totally alone here with the bears and bears aplenty. Saw 6 black bears today which included 2 cubs with momma. The first bear I saw, I thought was a cub, because it was on the side of the road down in a ditch like area. I stopped near it 30 feet away and started talking to it, asking it where it's momma was. All of a sudden, she jumped out on the road and I saw she was momma and she seemed non too happy I was talking to her like a baby. I left in a hurry, almost losing my camera again, though I did get a few pictures of the other bears. The best was a little fox on side of the road. I stopped nearby, shut engine off and it came right up to me only a few feet away and sat down. I talked to it for about 15 minutes until a car came down the road and beeped the horn at me as my bike was parked pretty much in the middle of the road on a corner. Not many vehicles out here but next time I'll try to get further off road.

Even though it rained a lot I absolutely loved the journey here again. So much wildlife. The lake only 10 feet from my tent is trampled with fresh (today) bear tracks in the sand/mud. I shouldn't have cancelled my biggest insurance policy until/if I get home. The "veteran" Aaron who's rode so far on his 500cc KTM dirt bike today was completely discouraged with the rain and cold, very negative and ready to give up. I on the other hand was supercharged with the beautiful day yesterday, so the rain didn't bother me a bit. He has not ridden through anything here that I haven't as we came from the same direction, Alaska – South. I tried to cheer him up, but he was completely "fed up". Oh well, guess I'm the new veteran on the block. He was going to try and come here but I haven't seen him. He actually drives faster than I do, as I'm trying not to get clobbered by wildlife jumping out on the road. Hope it's a beautiful day tomorrow since I'd love to stay here a few more days.

7/14/17

No plan to plan B

Another splendid day! I mean awesome! Had a little rain this morning which I slept through. Then the day broke warm and sunny in paradise. Highway 37A (alternate) and 200 miles in any direction is just breathtaking beauty. I truly could live here in a heartbeat during summer of course. I'd hate to bathe in the lakes and rivers in the winter, which many are froze over. Still seeing glaciers all along the ride on 37A. This morning I jumped in naked and bathed very quickly all alone in paradise! I so wish you were here all of you to enjoy, so we'll have to put that on everyone's bucket list. Today was sunny and warm. Needed no clothes not even a "shirt". I was planning on staying another night, but I knew it was Friday weekend with the locals who come to the lake to camp. I took my sweet time and finally left just short of 5pm. When I woke up everyone was gone, but a few cars trucks (3) came driving up and when they saw me alone, only wearing my thermal bottoms and boots, unzipped with all my clothes and gear drying on all the picnic tables and me looking like something out of the movie "Deliverance" they fled! I decided to clean up and take a bath, trim myself all up with the scissors and even exercise. For breakfast I ate dry granola, raisins and drank a V8 juice. Lunch was PB&J, banana and water. Dinner I stopped on side of highway just before I got to this campsite and made a sardine sandwich, cheddar chips and water. That's all but it works.

The reason I stopped to eat is to make sure to never eat especially sardines at camp site. Bears are no joke in these parts and a mistake could be your last. I always walk away from my campsite to eat a main meal. Sometimes, I eat a snack in the tent as long as I have nothing left over. I got sidetracked on my plan/intention to head back to Prince George where I was looking forward to using my "med. Card", but it is 8 hours away. I wasn't making it tonight with my leisurely departure time. When I got to Kitwanga, a very small town in Paradise, I was racing along this awesome highway with little to no cars, but potential trouble with wildlife and only to keep a guy on a Honda Goldwing from passing me as I again felt like being naughty. I met a local and "got sidetracked" David was riding a nice Harley when I pulled up at the only gas station for a long while and we started talking. Really nice guy, who both "medicated" me and gave me all I needed in Canada!

Dave told me about Terrace, a super scenic ride 1 ½ hours to the West in direction of Price Rupert. I'm not quite there yet, about 15 minutes since I got in too late, after 10pm. I will have to be more careful since I'm not allowing myself enough time to scout a safe enough campsite. I pulled into this provincial park campsite, but they wanted $20. I thought it was free which is my favorite price. The ranger told me about this spot on the next side of them up a hill, so that's where I am. Really not my best choice.

He said someone spotted a bear today there, and my tent is only 8 ft from the thickest dark woods you have ever seen. I don't particularly like it as I normally camp in the open as much as possible to have an earlier warning. This is definitely risky, but it's already dark. These last few camp sites I didn't walk anywhere without my gun or bear spray nearby. Not even to brush my teeth, but I'd rather not camp around people even though it's safer. That's what I get for not being "quite wite".

7/15/17

Epiphany

I feel so inspired and free on this journey. I've learned what I was always sure of and that's if once I set my mind to accomplish something, I won't stop until I do. I've also discovered I have the toughness to make it with very little and deal with whatever challenge comes my way and to do it alone (most of time) and in nature with all her dangers, my epiphany is "you" my love, Cheryl Moyce Tingler – I really love you so much and miss you and all the kids. How's that? An enigma too!

Today was a day of weather like St. Helena. Constant rain/sun/rain/sun/rain and more rain. Broke camp early as I noticed black clouds rolling in. Good thing since just as I was ready to leave the rain came. Better to break camp before everything is wet. I took my time and still made 350 miles or so and now just ½ hour or so from Prince George. Had a great breakfast and best deal yet on trip at a Holiday Inn in Terrace, BC. I pulled in just to really get under their overhung roof from the downpour. I paid $4 and ate great scrambled eggs, all I wanted, bacon, turkey and port sausage, hot oatmeal with walnuts and raisins, 2 bananas, chocolate milk and cranberry juice. I make up for my wilderness meals when I get a good deal like that. I decided to camp earlier than I normally would, around 6pm. A very ugly black sky was about to break loose and looked as though I would be in it for a long time, so even I have had enough today. Camp's free, right off road in rest area, but road isn't as busy as yesterday.

7/16/17

Back to Jasper/Alberta

Today a repeat of yesterday with even more rain. I'm still "supercharged" from that great day on 14th at Clements Lake where I was like "Adam and It" in Paradise. This cold and continuous rain, I'm sure turns back many a biker. I'm camped at Jasper National Park and it's packed with people. I got a site on the edge, more remote. This is also big time bear country, so I'll have to listen up at night. It's probably not helping that I'm eating M & Ms in my tent and it's dark outside. I don't plan on leaving any to share….that is. Bag does say "share size".

I tried to find a nice spot on a river and saw some but they were too visible to any passing park rangers who might chase me off. They only want you in designated camp grounds in this huge park. I had to pay $22, but I made sure I got my moneys worth in the hot shower. After all the cold rain, my 30 minute hot shower felt awesome. Now I'm good for 2 or 3 more days. I'm looking for free camp tomorrow. I'll probably look for another campsite on a remote site in this park. This place is awesome.

7/17/17

Found it! Super campsite!

If the park rangers find me here, they will surely run me off. Turns out Jasper and Banff are just one Big National Park that includes all the Columbia ice fields and glaciers and all this majestic beauty for 1000sq miles. It's big business as they want everyone's money to camp and have set about blocking off all access roads to the wilderness, glacial rivers and lakes. I've found a nice remote spot where 2 ice cold rivers merge surrounded by glacial mountains. Totally awesome, and all alone. This is only a few miles away from where I crashed going to Alaska.

It's about 50 miles south of last campsite in park. The "money section" of park. I saw the exact spot I wiped out at and as I suspected, the winds blow off the ice fields and glaciers just as you round the pass. I'm sure that contributed to the "wipeout" but no harm, no foul. I drove my Harley down some gravel paths well hidden from most anyone except the bears. As soon as I walked to the site I set up camp and heard some crashing in nearby woods and thought I saw a black bear. Well thinking is knowing. They're here all right and I love being all alone out here. People irritate me for the most part. When I'm camping I 'd definitely rather be alone, unless my family were here. The people are super nice, it's just that "when I drink alone, I like to be all by myself" (George Thorogood song). I hope to stay put here a few days. Before I left last camp, I took another 30 minute hot shower that morning, knowing it'll be a few days before any hot water comes my way again. Plenty cold right here!

7/18/17

Cold and smoke: Plan B again

Last night on this glacial campsite, I completely froze. It was the coldest night yet and colder than my time in Alaska. Fellow named Rich from Nebraska with his old buddy Brewster on pedal bikes said it was 31 degrees F where they just came from, but I was further north then them and in the icefield areas. 3 long sleeves/thermals in bag did very little. Hard to sleep and kept thinking about "buddy bear" So far bears not interested in me. This camp site's also in their backyard and ice cold stream 10ft away flow into nearby lake. I'm only 30 miles from US border I crossed in Montana. I would loved to stay at last site, inspite of cold, but next morning the visibility was reduced to 1/1/2 miles of smoke and haze from the 200 plus fires still burning West of here, hundreds of miles away. This is a really nice beautiful spot and I may stay an extra day. Everyone I meet is extremely nice. I didn't realize I rode as far as I did today and so I wanted one nice camp in Canada. This is it!

When I realized the US border was only 30 miles away I saw a sign pointing to a lake and off I went. Pulled into a remote campsite on lake but the road down to it was very steep with dirt and gravel so I parked up the hill and started walking down. A vehicle with 2 Canadian girls and a guy and a baby girl came along and told me that it was full and I had to pay. They then told me about this site 4 miles away and free. They even drove ahead of me here while I followed them. That's what I mean about how friendly everyone I meet, especially in Canada and Alaska are. I probably would have missed it as these are remote areas. Happy Anniversary, tomorrow (coupla hours from now) Kyle and Annalise! Your 5th Anniversary....I think! Congratulations! Well for the record, I entered Canada on Father's Day and may return to US tomorrow on kids Anniversary. A little over a month and some 7000 miles. About 2 weeks each in Canada and Alaska. It's truly been an awesome experience up here alone. Thank you, babe for supporting me! <3

7/19/17

Canada one more day! Happy Anniversary, Kyle and Annalise!

All alone again in nice camp spot as the 2 fellows Rick and Brewster left to follow Rockies on Bicycles, south to New Mexico through Rockies. Love this free camp site. Spent several hours today plotting out and writing down the rest of my intended route to home sweet home! I've plotted most all "backroads" entire way with only small areas of interstate, unavoidable without major detours. Should be home by end of August. Fixing to take ice cold mountain stream bath and enjoy this beautiful sunny, warm day. Off to America tomorrow. Montana only ½ hour away to see Lloyd and Deanna again. Been spectacular!

I'm really enjoying a completely leisurely day. No one here but me except a local fire chief came by to make sure no fires, as "ban" is on everywhere and a good thing. Nothing like an ice cold bath to build character and scream "LIFE", do what you got to and love it! I'm recharging my "cells" again on this great sunny warm day. Been in my blue baggies all day. No shirt, no shoes, no cares. I got in some long overdue exercising and feel really well. Haven't left camp since arriving. Been eating very well, granola, raisins, bananas, PB&Js, oat bars, sardines, broccoli and BBQ fritos!

7/22/17

Recharged again at "Allens"

Timing is everything in life. Good thing I stayed an extra day camping in Canada, as Lloyd and Deanna had some dozen grand/great grand children overnight on Wed and had just left. Got to meet Caroline, their daughter and her friend Freita, her two girls and 8 year old Payton. Had another great stay thanks to their kindness and all set for the second leg of this journey before home. Lloyd was very interested in my travels through Canada and Alaska and we talked a lot about "Writing Stone" and St. Helena. Lloyd and Deanna have seen our home there.

I am now camping just outside the Glacier National Park that was completely full in all campgrounds, not that I intended on camping in those. I've become pretty adept at searching out nice camp spots. This one was readymade, evident that someone did a lot of work to make this site. It's surrounded by several ice cold, clear creeks and steep mountains all around. Across the other side of the highway was another State Park on same "Devils Creek" here just south of Glacier. I was diligently searching for a spot on either lake or river with a road, to no avail, and finally saw a gravel road. I crossed the "Highway to Sun", the pass over center of mountain and only recently open because it was still closed for snow removal when I went through to Canada a month ago. Of course beautiful mountains so steep, still with snow. However, I know know Glacier Park here in Montana is spectacular, but it's small scale to BC and Alaska and the Dawson Range was like 10 Glacier Parks!

This camp site has a dug in rock fire pit, stacked firewood, wind break and situated in a big stand of trees. Really nice and I may stay here 2 days and then head for Kalispel about an hour from here and get 2 new tires and oil change at the HD shop. That will be approximately Tuesday morning. I'm over 11,000 miles now on trip and estimate another 4-5 thousand miles to go. Talked to Bob today and he said the "get-together" party with Scott and family at Neal's with our kids was nice. The cobia they ate sure sounded good. Hope everyone's enjoying Diane's baby shower today!

7/24/17

Too much noise – Too many people!

So plan B again! The noise from road traffic was so loud, the creeks couldn't drown it out. Lots of tourists all through the night driving to and from Glacier Park, and a constant train running up the mountain forced my hand. Nice camp site, but I like peace and quiet camping, and that's what I have now, but at a price $5. In the Bitteroot National Forest recreation site on Bass Creek, between Montana and Idaho. Great spot, ice cold, fast flowing, super clear creek I took my bath in today. I got here yesterday, thanks to missing my turn onto hwy 12 West to Oregon. Good thing as I had rode a few hundred miles with a usual late start and by the time I found this about ½ hour before dark, I was rapidly running out of options. This was perfect, plus today I was able to run back to Missoula and get 2 new tires, back brakes and oil change. "Bruce" is ready to rock and roll with Easy Rider X2 thanks to Grizzly Harley-Davidson. Was thinking about making Sturgis today, but decided the extra 2-3 thousand miles not worth it.

7/26/17

Mountain Man to City Slicker & Back

Broke camp for Oregon via Washinton with "Bruce" running good and looking good from the cleaning I gave it back at Lloyd and Deanna's. The ride for first 200 miles was super scenic mountainous through the Nez Perez territory that follows the Lewis & Clark trail along the ice cold, fast flowing, shallow, rocky, "Clear River" (it's name) in Idaho. As soon as I passed Lewiston West bound, I knew it was going to be hard to find anywhere to camp. Rode another 200 + miles through treeless, hilly land and no rivers that was all industrial and agricultural farm land, such as walla walla onions for miles on end. Although I started searching early for a site there was nothing to be found, just lots of people and realitively big cities. You couldn't pay me enough to live here long, and so I did run "sure enough" out of options and well after dark. I saw a sign to a RV park in Kennewick Pasco. A city of slickers, stores and restaurants by the hundreds and felt as out of place as a fish in the desert. However, after riding over 400 miles with temperatures at 104 F, even I had lost my sense of humor and mind…. I stopped at the RV park and noticed it was very noisy as it was along the highway and they wanted $30. A shower would would've been nice for that price, but that's all. A late working, maintenance worker pointed to a stand of what appeared to be the only trees in the city, behind several restaurants such as Subway, Mexican, Pizza, etc., and said he'd seen other "homeless" people camping there and if I was lucky, the cops won't catch me"! So there I was, Mr. Wilderness Mountain Man on a Harley that had slept among bears, reduced to competing with the "homeless"!

My guess is I fit right in. Only the Harley helped ease my worries. Most people gave me a wider berth than the homeless. I woke up to people whizzing by in their cars looking at "poor me" sticking out like a sore thumb with my red tent in the big city, behind the restaurants in the only stand of trees, and realized it's really only one small step to poverty. Note to myself, "don't lose Harley Bruce)! I literally waited behind several homeless men washing up in the gas station store bathroom, to do the same and felt right at home, but I wasn't kidding myself and wished they all had Harley's too! Anyway I had another epiphany to title this journey and journal "Homeless to Homer on Harley and Home". That's also an enigma and another Joe story!

7/27/17

Back to Mountain Man

Well the good news was after riding some 20 miles I left the city behind and was right back into the canyons and rivers of the cascade range in Washington. I continued for only a little over and hour and found a remote camp site along the icy cold river in a great stand of spruce trees with deer and other tracks all over that I think is mountain lion. They are all fresh and I'm back to being right at home all alone in these canyons. Awesome! Just had icy cold, well needed bath and am still naked as it's hot again.

This place is great and I may look to camp at Mt. Ranier, the 14,000 + mountain, some 30 miles from here as I'm crossing the cascade range over White Pass. I'm perfectly happy here and I have a really nice deep hole in the icy river to bath. It's totally awesome in this heat and I plan another dip or 2 before I leave. Today is a text book example of how to enjoy the freedom of the journey with no time consistencies, artificially imposed such as Patty and Jay were living. No schedule, no place to be and no time to get there!

7/28/17

White Pass, Hwy 12 – Mt. Rainier, WA

It's been another beautiful day, not as hot but sunny. I reluctantly broke camp in that awesome spot I found, but not before another ice cold bath in alpine river water and after exercising and eating PB&J wich and apple juice, around 1pm. I made it to White Pass which weaves between the Cascade Mountain Range with Mt. Rainier on right side West bound and Mt. St. Helens on left. This campsite is on a lake between mountains but can't see Mt. Rainier from here. I rode up to Rainier Nat'l Park, looking for campsites, only 10 miles from White Pass. I saw Mt. Rainier in very clear and cloudless weather today and she's as majestic and dangerous as snow covered volcanoes go. A really great, carefree day in beautiful country and so I only made about 20 miles today. I'm in no hurry to leave this area. I never saw anyone at my last site for over a day and only a few people here. Met "Grizzly" today with a dyed "red" haired girl from SSI (Brunswick, Ga.). Apparently they just came off the Pacific Coast Trail that runs the Rockies all the way from S. America, Mexico through N. America. They came walking up with backpacks to look for more provisions, I guess. He said he has walked it 3 times complete, both directions and the Appalachian Trail, twice. Maybe I'll try that someday. I certainly don't mind walking or being on my own, but I can't wait to be spoiled again, so I'll just have to see what boss lady has to say. Anyway, off to Oregon Coast tomorrow after cruising Mt. Rainier hwy.

7/30/17

Washington/ Oregon

Seems I lost track of time again. College kids I camped with informed me it's Sunday, 30th July 2017. I thought it was Friday. I was hoping to be alone at this really remote site on a mountain in the Siuslaw National Forest in a place called the Cumming Creek Wilderness. It's another really awesome area. I had to ride 2-3 miles up a steep gravel road to the trailhead areas that go up over the mountain. In parts you see over the Pacific Ocean and is super scenic. These college kids were all really nice, from across America, DC, Maryland, Mich and Oregon studying to be doctors, engineers and archeologists. All the state forest camp grounds along the coast are full and they charge up to $30 per night, which of course, I wanted nothing to do with. I was alone to near dark or beyond when they came driving up. Just as well since this site was really "bear looking wilderness" with elk signs all over. We had fun hanging out and listening to "Joe stories". I was planning to stay another day, but realize I'm running behind schedule to see Kyle in Nevada and Sturgis by 10th or so of August.

Camped on a lake in White Pass near Mt. Rainier on 7/29/17 and then rode through the Steven's canyon Gorge, a 60 mile ride through the Mt. Rainier National Park or what's called Paradise Highway. Super scenic and every bit as spectacular as Glacier National Park. I coasted into the only gas station around with only "fumes" left in my tank. The computer readout on Bruce showed I only had less than 10 miles on tank which had stopped reading after I continued on another 5 miles or so. Luckily I found a station in time. I then continued on through rolling hills and farm land that unlike, Lewiston, ID., this farm land had trees. Had to camp at a "people" RV park with me being the only tent among expensive RVs, but the place had heated indoor pool, hot baths and laundry, so I sacrificed the $29. I was late arriving in the RV site once again. That was in Washington State and miles from Border of Oregon and Pacific Ocean. Rode to this site along hwy 101, Pacific Coast Hwy on 29th looking for a campsite, but too many tourists are swamping the state parks along the beaches. So now I'm off to the Siskiyou National Forest in Southern Oregon a few hours south of here. Camping in National Forests are free. The Cascades are beautiful and the beaches and ocean very scenic.

7/31/17

Reluctantly left Cumming Creek Wilderness, but no choice as I was out of drinking water. Had to ride both brakes off mountain and gravel road. Been giving Bruce a real workout and no doubt took an extra 500 miles of tread off my new tires. Met more interesting and nice people along the way. Rode on over 200 miles and didn't realise it was further inland and next thing I know I'm at a border "agriculture" Checkpoint station for California. I was already running late into the evening and only ½ hour before dark and was looking forward to camping another night in Oregon. I said "hello and good bye, California", wheeled old Bruce around and pointed him back to Oregon looking for a remote site. Fortunately I spotted a small old sign showing a camp that I turned down once back in Oregon. There was no mileage given on the camp so I kept going on an awesome winding road through forest and well kept homes and ranches. I ended up driving some 40 miles before I finally found the camp site. It's very remote in the forest but a very popular camp for the locals. No one else would every know it's here. It's awesome, scenic, peaceful and my spot is only 30 ft above an ice cold mountain stream, full of rainbow trout. Water's nice and clear. I'm having a nice time, here recuperating. Felt really tired this morning so decided quite easily to stay another day rent free, with awesome scenery and free bath! I really relaxed and slept late, exercised down by the stream where the rocks are smooth and there was the only branch that swung back and forth but worked for pull-ups, that is. Only getting to exercise once or twice a week, sometimes because I can't find proper branch. While I was doing pushups on the rocks, only about 3 ft above the water, I was watching pan size rainbow trout swim by. Don't want to leave tomorrow, but I'm down to only a few ounces of drinking water. Tomorrow I go back to California where I'll be in the Redwood Forest within an hour. First I have to drive out of this 3-4 mile gravel road in the mountains. I'll try to see Kyle on the weekend of August 4th. I'm going to feel like s fish out of water in Vegas!

8/1/17

California Redwoods

Got an early start for me and broke camp and on the road by 915am. Twenty minutes or so later I'm back in California. The redwood forests are quite large, so I spent most of the day walking and riding through the redwoods of both Jediah State Park, only a few miles inside California Border with the beautiful Smith river and others flowing through the park and the Red Wood National Park around 80 miles further South of Jediah. Always wanted to touch and gaze awestruck at 2000+ year old and some 250 ft tall trees. I really enjoyed what little I got to see which was hundreds of giant red wood, but if I had time and security of motorcycle I would walk (love to) endlessly among the giants. Totally awesome. Jehovah's creation and to think that Methusala who lived so long, still lived less than ½ the life of these giants, and us the oldest human today is a baby in a redwood life! There's trailheads everywhere to walk through the forest for miles on end. Wish you were here to walk with me, my dear Cheryl and kids!

I would have loved to stay back at Jediah Park as there were remote sites along the beautiful river to camp at, but I knew I also wanted to see the even bigger, taller redwoods in the park some 80 miles south. So to save a day on time, I reluctantly continued on and sure enough missed out on where I would much rather have camped. As it turned out, there was nowhere further south to camp without paying, so there goes my $25 and my wilderness site is now a RV park called Elk Ranch. It's actually not bad as I needed another shower even though I had an ice cold stream bath yesterday, but everything's hot and dry here and very dusty. Still, I'd much prefer the cold, beautiful streams and rivers to bathe in for free! This camp site is on a peaceful flowing creek, right behind my tent. Today I saw a herd of elk and took pictures. A bear and mountain lion were sighted in this camp apparently today. Another lady showed me a picture she took of a track she didn't know. It was bear and she said it was only a little distance down the road.

8/3/17

Temperatures today over 100 F and snow

Rode some 300 miles yesterday and was not doing well mentally, which I never seem to do on the 31st anniversary of my dad passing away. Too many sad memories. Anyway, I camped last night in a RV park again, except this time it was free, because I couldn't find the attendants to pay. It was nice enough on a lake and canal in mountainous country called Clearlake, CA. The route I've taken through CA is really pretty nice. Lots of very nice canyon roads, windy, hilly and no traffic. None too exciting long, straight stretches for 50 miles of agriculture. Fields of peach trees and all sorts of vegetables and then back to awesome canyon roads. Missed quite a few turns today going 20 miles out of my intended path due to poorly marked highways in CA. Temperatures this morning was really nice and cool til around 10am. It then by noon climbed steadily over 100 F and stayed that way. I got to Yosemite on the Tioea Pass some 10,000 ft up and now with snow.

Make no mistake that even on a motor bike, you have to be tough to deal with the extreme temperature and weather fluctations daily, even hourly. You need to become as proficient at setting up camp in the dark as I have already several times this week, including tonight and last night due to covering a lot of miles and running late. I probably rode over 400 miles today in getting to Yosemite and camped in mountain pass 10,000ft up. Beautiful, magnificient scenery and back to wearing thermals after sweating in the extreme heat today!

8/5/17

So you see, I'm in a hurry now to see my baby, Moycey Poo" as she is flying into Vegas tomorrow to see me and Kyle and Annalise. Can't wait to see everyone again and wish Coco, Troy, little Everett Joe, Travis, Diane and little, little Tallulah Rose could also be there. Better get on my poker face ☺ Expecting more really nice riding tomorrow for a few hours through Yosemite mountains before the brutal desert heat of California and Nevada hit me hard. Got to take the good with the bad and so looking forward to Vegas!

8/8/17

Busted in Vegas

Hello Journal! A lot has happened since limping into Las Vegas. Departed last camp in Yosemite on Aug 4 enroute to Vegas and definitely uncertain on route I chose. I've never been in these parts and I know there's a good or better way and a bad way through desert land on a bike. Fortunately I used the tried and true method of asking locals and I quickly revised my intended route which would have been a big mistake, since it was through Death Valley, California, the oven, but the most direct to Vegas. I took a recommended pass through some of the most awesome canyon roads and super scenery and over 10,000 ft into the Ancient Bristle Cone Pine Forest on Hwys 168 & 266. It was an amazing experience and as good as the best riding and scenic roads of the journey. I crossed the Sierra Nevada and White Mountains (Coco Sierra's name place) and sort of stumbled upon the road leading to the Ancient Forest. I couldn't resist detouring for a few hours going into the most awe inspiring forest of trees and oldest living things on earth at nearly 5000 years old! Mind boggling!

I found what I believed would be most oldest or way up there and because I was alone as a thunderstorm with hail had been underway and keeping others away, I decided to climb up to the tree off the designated trail. Just had to! This ancient tree had a perfect horizontal branch for pull ups and I felt so inspired just being there at over 10,000ft and underneath, holding onto one of the oldest living things on earth that I did 22 pullups with boots and raingear on. I completely surprised myself as I'd never done more than 16 that I can remember. Not bad for an old timer tree, at 4000 years plus and a baby at 60! Had the rangers spotted me they would surely have booted me out of the park and maybe what surprised me most was how awesome (my favorite overused word) and how much fun the driving was on all these roads right through California and especially from before Yosemite and all the way to Vegas. However, before I made it to Vegas and out on a long, straight stretch of desert, old Bruce broke down. Very bad timing and situation since this stretch of highway is rarely traveled and I only saw about 5 or 6 vehicles in the hour or more I was stranded. My throttle cables and grip fell apart and left me with no throttle. The temperature was rising above 90 F at around 2pm in the afternoon. I realized my situation was nearly as bad as it gets when it comes to being in the "middle of nowhere", with only a small bottle of water and a quick prayer I sent up. Finally, along came a car. I asked them to call for help when they got to the next closest town/store, also in the middle of nowhere and some 75 miles away. They gave me their last cold water and coke and proceeded to let me know that I wasn't making Vegas tonight! Duh! However, I had an ace up my sleeve, which was an ernest, desperate prayer for a fix. Sure enough, within moments, I started trying to take a closer look at the problem and then began yanking at the cables which separated the throttle from it's housing and allowed me enough cable to manually pull the throttle to move forward. It was clumsy and hard and half the time I used both hands on the throttle cable on the right side of handlebar to pull the cable enough to maintain speed. It worked enough to travel like that for the next 300 to 4oo miles limping along in what could have been the most horrible environment you never want to be in. A near disaster turned out way better than could have been anticipated as the temperature cooled down due to overcast skies and the roads were great and scenic all into Vegas. Here I am to meet my lovely wife, Cheryl who flew into Vegas on same day, I almost didn't make and Kyle and Annalise who we haven't seen in a long while. I've had a nice stay with them and Cheryl even though it was a very busy time for Kyle and Annalise who were just setting up and moving into their very nice new apartment. Bruse is in Red Rock Harley awaiting overnight cables and throttle grips and I'm lounging about the pool and gym waiting to get on the road home, but first Sturgis last 2 days of motorcycle rally.

8/9/17

Back in the saddle

After some anxious moments for me on Tuesday awaiting parts that still hadn't arrived by 3pm and me chomping at the bit to get going, UPS finally shows up about 2 hours before closing and I luck out! Although I had a lot of fun with Kyle, Annalise and Momma Ting and love the set up of kids apartment, I was also anxious to complete the journey and put the icing on the cake, by celebrating in Sturgis. I can taste the finish line….home, and will be excited to arrive safely. Good fortune out of almost complete despair is continuing. I got up at 4am to beat the heat of Nevada and Utah heading NNE and was rolling down the highway, my earliest ever at 7am. Not sure where the other 3 hours went to. Sure can't blame Patty and Jay! Nevertheless, Mr. Turtle is winning the race, having done 450 miles today riding at an average speed of 75 – 80 MPH on wide open and little traveled interstates I15 and I70 to Denver. The weather was cooler than expected so the ride was most comfortable and scenic. This time of year Nevada and Utah could hit the 120 F temperatures, but I'm so grateful it was in the low 80s. I blew by my intended campsite some 200 miles back on Fish Lake Indian Reservation in some beautiful mountainous land and stumbled upon an awesome….again….camp ground more than 10 miles off the interstate. I have become very reliant on word of mouth by locals, no matter how they look. By 5pm I was getting tired and stopped at a gas station in the small, middle of nowhere town in the plains of canyons called Green River. An ole country boy, who mumbled with what few teeth he had, overheard me asking a police officer who drove up, about campsites. The officer was very friendly, but not a local like ole country boy who proceeded to tell me about 3 or 4 separate times about this remote campsite. It's on Green River which is really a muddy brown, very fast flowing river through the canyons. My camp site is absolutely great with nice trees and right beside big rapids. It's near identical to the canyons I hiked with Kyle and Annalise in Nevada and very peaceful and scenic and dangerous. Not from animals this time, but from floods. I traveled down rocky dirt and gravel roads again to get here and both the local and signs warn of flashfloods. If a big thunderstorm hit here, one would be lucky to get away with their life. The ole country boy warned me to get out if it rains. I can see why. So what I mistakenly thought the exciting part of the journey was over, it seems to keep staying as good as ever. When I complete this journey I've decided to nickname myself, Journeyman Joe. I'm no longer a rookie and it's been a epic journey. The great baseball coach and legend Yogi-Bera says "It ain't over 'til it's over"! ☺

8/10/17

Back to High Mountain Passes

Last night the winds and rain came fast out of the canyon and shook my tent everywhere and ripped my rainfly off. Wind felt like 50MPH or more with me and all my gear in the tent, I didn't fly away. Fortunately it was short lived or I would have been trapped in that area. Got an early start and on road by 830am, cruising at mostly 80 MPH on I70 towards Denver East bound. I mapped out another fantastic pass through the Rocky Mountains, turning North some 50 miles before Denver. In high altitudes over 10,000ft last 100 miles or more on route I haven't been on. That's saying something since I feel like I've been on every high hountain pass in N. America. Seen two big bull moose grazing on side of road and also a big porcupine. Made some 380 miles today and I'm camped high up on a mountain pass in Arapaho Natational Forest alone at over 10, 000ft. It's awesome and recent bear sightings posted both on boards and a neon sign, including date. So I don't know how much sleep I'll get tonight as I'm definitely back in the bear playgrounds. Of course I gave away the only can I had left of bear spray yesterday, to a girl who was driving a very old car on the Interstate out of Nevada. I passed her on my bike and thought that was risky, driving a car like that in the middle of nowhere as that interstate was. At least if you break down other cars come by, but it could be very dangerous for someone alone and no protection. So I stopped at a rest stop for scenic photo and she also pulled in. We talked and she was scared her car wouldn't make it and when I offered her the bear mace, she was grateful, saying she shouldn't have risked the long drive across the desert in the bomber. The mace had been given to me by a lady from Australia in Homer, Alaska and now passed onto a lady again. Tonight my shot gun is back by my side and I'm back to wearing thermals, as the temperatures will probably be in the 40s tonight! Bye!

8/11/17

Sturgis, Maybe Tomorrow!

Broke camp late, around 1030am to catch up on rest. No bear last night, but very cold. Met a guy named Brian and Kiwi his dog. Says he's been living out of his truck mostly last 10 years moving from one National Forest to another every 2 weeks or so. Law does not allow a person to camp longer at one time. Had another great ride through windy canyon roads for over 100 miles or so including taking hwy 34 across the Rocky Mountain National Park in Colorado. Named the Adjetives for grandeur and you would be right! Such a spectacular, amazing, rocky mountain high! I think it was the highest pass I crossed including Alaska, as the road went spiraling up over 12,000 ft and closer to 13000,ft. After crossing summit and Rocky Mountain divide, the road continued awesome for some 50 miles of super steep, high, rocky canyons, though very dangerous with rock falls. Rode on for another 2000 miles or so through high, windy, plains of Wyoming. Sturgis further than I thought as I've already traveled more than 1,100 miles since leaving Kyle and Annalise in Nevada and have another 150 miles or more tomorrow to get there. Seeing that it was an hour or less to dark and I hadn't had a bath in 3 days, I spotted a sign in Lusk, Wyoming to BJ's campground. It was an excellent choice, because she has a 5 star bathroom. Completely luxurious, hot water, towel and fresh pillows. Stayed in about an hour and for $20 well worth it to camp. Of course, I did wash my face and some of my body 2 days ago in the muddy water of Green River. So off to celebrate my journey in Sturgis tomorrow for sure! Wish you were here babe! One more week lover girl <3

8/14/17

Sturgis and Home

Left BJ's campground with another morning shower, getting my $20 worth, as it may be my last for a while until I find a lake or river. Rode into Sturgis on Saturday for the last hurrah! Smiling and ready to celebrate my 1st Sturgis ever on it's last big day of it's 77th Anniversary. I must have set a record of sorts as I rode over 15,000 miles and 9 weeks to get to my first and maybe last Sturgiss motorcycle rally at age 60. Now that's an epic adventure for a young man! Well it didn't take very long before I was cornered by a couple of middle age women who had me out on a dance floor with my shirt off. Of course and vodka flowing, doing the limbo while the crowd was cheering and a great jam being played by a band from Nashville. These gals, my age, most likely a lot younger kept wanting to party with me so they showed me how to get into the outdoor jam festival at a place called Buffalo Chips, which was 3 miles down the road from Main Street, Sturgis. There I set up camp out in the middle of this wide open field that could have held up to 500 thousand RV campers, but with only one other tent camper out there, while we listened to Blue Oyster Cult and other bands jam away though the night. Since I had followed these women here and it was after 10pm and I had already been partying since arriving at noon, I was content to just listen to the music from my lonesome camp in the big field. I could hear the thousands of people cheering and hollering and bikes racing and doing burn outs. I didn't realize what a huge event it was having set up after dark and couldn't see the area well, but when I woke up in the morning there were thousands of RV campers a mile or two away and the place was immense in size and acres. The 2 women were real characters, but very nice, although I think they were hoping I would let them sleep in the tent, which wasn't happening. One was called Carol Sue and she was like a left over flower child from the 60s and San Franscisco with the flowers in her long hair. She kept dancing in circles and throwing her hair all around. She was a dancer and was the one doing the limbo while we danced on stage at one of the saloons on Main Street upon meeting them. Her friend called herself "Salty" and she claimed to be a radio talk show host who has her own show and wants me to star in it with all my "Joe Stories". She had her camera and was filming and videoing me all night. They were traveling in a van and were gone in the morning when I woke up, and I think a little miffed I wouldn't let them sleep in my tent. It had been fun and after breaking camp and riding the 3 miles back to Sturgis, Sunday morning, I brought a couple shirts, had breakfast and realized I was down to a grand total of $99 and change to last me the next 200 miles or so home and another week of traveling. I'm not the slightest bit worried since I've become very adept at living free and for free. I've got enough nut, granola, PB&J and sardines to last me 3 or 4 days and maybe enough gas money to limp into Georgia if not Florida. By then, I'm hoping it will be pay day and I can get the rest of the way home. If anybody can do it, I know I can! Homeless on a Harley, to Homer and Home and loving it! So I rode on for about 350 miles and there was no suitable place to camp the whole way for free as I was in the treeless hills and plains of South Dakota and no rivers or lakes to be seen. I amended my intended route and aimed for the Missouri River on the Southern border of South Dakota and the Northern border of Nebraska. I arrived about an hour or so before dark, crossed the Missouri River on hwy 18 East and spotted the only nice stand of trees along the highway that was up a grassy hill overlooking a valley near the river. I was in the Dakota, Sioux Indian Reservation lands. I turned toward that potential camp site and parked. I would have to walk it to see if my Harley could get up the grassy forested slope and be hidden from passers by. A female Sheriff promptly spotted me and pulled up next to me. She wanted to know what I was doing and basically told me to get moving out of her town, to which I said "Yes Mam"! She dutifully stooped down to look at my license plate to check my current registration and says to me, "Well I see you have a current license plate, so I guess I don't need to be talking to you anymore, and you'll be on your way". I waited until she was out of sight and then climbed the hill into the woods and realized it was a great camp site if I could get the Harley up there and hide ourselves. Old Bruce and I have been doing some off roading and although a bit risky and unproven terrain, we made it and camouflaged the chrome from Ms. Sheriff. It's been a great camp site, but now it's morning and breaking this camp in search of the National Forests of Missouri, where it's both legal to camp for free and hopefully I'll find a nice river or lake to bathe in. I'll pass on the Missouri river as Ms. Sheriff may notice me in her town.

8/16/17

Good Fortune continues!

I rode out of my hiding spot, Monday morning of Aug 15th and back tracked across the Missouri River and soon spotted an excellent spot to swim and bathe in the Missouri, by a boat launch where only 3 vehicles with boat trailers were parked. No one was there and I was able to get a well needed bath and swim. I continued on through Nebraska North to South and then at Southern end of Nebraska I rode on Eastward, covering near the entire state which was all cattle and corn. Literally hundreds of miles of nothing but corn as far as you can see and a few people and cars. The scenery was better than I expected as Nebraska was gently rolling, green hill country and the weather was pleasant and not very hot for middle of August. Covered another 350 miles and again nowhere to camp except in the middle of some farmer's corn field. Now it was one hour after dark and I figured I'd be riding past midnight and into Missouri before finding any good camp site. I was already quite tired, so I stopped at a gas station in the very small farming town of Washington, Kansas and asked the girl running the station if by chance there was any campground nearby that were free. I was down to $34 after my fill up and Jehovah answered my prayer I sent up some 15 minutes earlier to help me find a good camp spot. The girl said "Sure, just around the corner at end of next road to left". What a great site to camp for free. I'm on a lovely mowed, grassy, knoll surrounded by big, beautiful trees (finally(and it's a proper RV campground with full electric, water, bathrooms, showers and a swimming pool and I'm the only persone here. Talking about the power of prayer, I'm so incredibly grateful! I'm tempted to stay another day as it's so peaceful and lovely here and the weather is beautiful. How lucky, for the middle of August in Kansas can be brutally hot. Anyway, I may set off today after my exercise, bath and then very leisurely departure to the Mark Twain National Forests of the Missouri Ozarks ☺

8/17/17

Back to Missouri Ozarks

Reluctantly departed the only campground so miraculously found and for at least 300 miles in any direction. There is nowhere else but cornfields and no water and few trees. I rode on for 300 miles, leaving at my leisurely time of 215pm as I was enjoying the recuperating and peace of little ole Washington, Kansas, and sure enough another 300 miles of same agriculture belt as Nebraska and Kansas and Missouri. Next to prison, I couldn't imagine living in such places where there is little water or trees and only corn and cows to keep you company. The good news continues as I made it to a very small section of the Mark Twain National Forest, I spotted on the atlas, South of Colombia, Missouri, and especially since it was again almost dark and the next big section of this forest is another 100 miles south of here. I stopped in a gas station and asked a local brother, if he knew of any campgrounds in this area, and he pointed me down the road not on my atlas, but what I suspected was one leading into this small section of forest and again just what I needed in time. A great ride through rolling green timbered hills for about 8 – 10 miles and here lies a free National Forest campground with everything but showers and only a few people 3 – 4 including me. I hope to break camp here later today, awaiting weather to clear as we just had a thunderstorm and head just south of Rolla, Misssouri where there's a much bigger section of the National Forest and streams and rivers through that area. I usually and much prefer just being out in the woods and not a designated campground even if it's free. Coasting on fumes., now! Arriving with $7 and a dollar or two in change and a mostly full tank! All's well as I'm only 1500 miles from home and I have 3-4 days worth of food in my saddlebag. That is if you call dinner sardine sandwiches and PB&Js and other assorted non perishable snacks. Now if I can only find a mountain, high enough that I can coast in neutral most the way home, and if not, and likely not, then I only neeed to wait another day or 2 until pay day, and poor mama Ting will have never seen such a poor, scraggly looking man, as me come driving up. Sure hope she gets to cooking me something up right away to help put some meat back on my bones. When I arrived in this camp with only 20 minutes or so before dark, I pulled Bruce over to my site and parked on the grass. A man across the way named Jeff was happy to see me arrive on a Harley as he was retired Army and a biker as well. He offered me a nice, cold Coors beer which I can only remember drinking 2 – 3 beers at most on this journey and we chatted at his campsite until another 20 minutes after dark. I go set up or start to set up my camp when this man camping in another area walks up to me in the dark with his shirt open and wearing a knife around his neck and tells me he is with the Forestry Dept and that I can't park Bruce on the grass in front of my site. Apparently he didn't realize I'm a Journeyman and always keep old Bruce right next to me. I told him, "Ole Bruce stays with me and I've been traveling for 2 ½ months and I'm tired and good night, Mister"! He insisted being a butthead and told me, "It's the rules and if I don't listen. This place will be crawling with park rangers in the morning"! I again told him, "I don't care and goodnight Mister"! He starts to slowly walk away, until I chambered 5, 12 gauge shotgun rounds in which he clearly heard and I never heard from or seen him again. Something tells me he wasn't as stupid as he looked! Well it's off to the next section of these Ozarks and I can't wait to find another clear, cold mountain stream if the U. S. Treasury hasn't run out of paper money and I get paid by Friday, I should be in Florida by Saturday.

8/18/17

Ozarks and Tornado County

Woke up to thunderstorms, lightning and heavy rain. I waited til what I thought was a good enough break in the action and broke camp for a larger section of the National Forest with rivers, some 100 miles south of here. Timing was everything and I no sooner got a mile or two down the road and all hell broke loose. Lightning was everywhere, little bits of hail was bouncing off my helmet and a very heavy rain. So with another prayer to Jehovah as it was quite scary, I made it safely to a gas station and parked in the middle of the pump overhang. Lots of cars were also pulling off and trying to get under it but I had the best spot right in the middle. Some folks were kind enough to pull up radar weather on their phones and it showed embedded thunderstorms rolling through the area for most of the day, so I stayed there about an hour waiting for a break I saw on the radar. The wind was blowing at least 50 MPH and rain driving horizontal with lightning cracking everywhere and had all appearances of a tornado about to spin off. Fortunately after an hour it subsided long enough for me to get going and I rode in a light rain most of the way to exactly what I was looking for on the atlas. It showed the forest and river area but not the numerous little country roads leading to it. I just kept working the roads for about 15 – 20 miles in the area I knew it was and eventually found another great campsite right on the river and way out in the boonies. I'm the only one here and it's quiet, peaceful and beautiful. Ole Bruce is right here on the grass beside my tent and no Rambo, forestry man to tell me foolishly where to park. No sooner than I got here I had to work fast to get camp set as it was getting dark and the thunderstorms were approaching fast. All night there was lots of rain and lightning. Woke up to a beautiful day so far and a tent with puddles of water in it. All's good as I have a river to bathe in and I still have $2 in change left.

8/19/17

Uncle Sam to the Rescue

I'm actually not sure of the day since my cell phone seldom works and my non smart phone, otherwise known to me as my dumb ass flip phone with a kick start due to old technology is unreliable. That's okay, because I'm kicking and Bruce is purring and we'll be home soon, before the snow falls! Been riding now for 2 days since breaking camp in the Ozarks on the Big Piney River. That was definitely my last boonie campsite before megatropolis sets in. Rode some 800 miles in two days, camping last night on Reel Foot Lake in NW Tennessee, that was created as a result of an earthquake, supposedly. The riding was mostly boring to me as all the great scenery is behind me. The good news that kept me cheerful was the weather stayed good and pleasant for August. I was not happy with the poor road signage in both Missouri and Tennessee, nor California. It's quite ridiculous when you travel some 50 miles or more before you see a highway number sign and you've passed by lots of different roads. So I definitely got lost a few times, ended up on the wrong highway 51 in Missouri where there was another different highway 51 and not that far away from the other completely different hwy 51 which led me into Nowhere'sville, Arkansas, I did not want to be in. I had seen enough cornfields to last me a lifetime through Oklahoma, Kansas, Nebraska and Missouri right into Tennessee. So it's no fun backtracking 50 miles through endless cornfields, then the only campsite due to endless cornfields being 30 miles in the wrong direction, but I chose the out of the way camp on Reel Foot Lake or be driving after dark for hours before finding another suitable area.

There I was able to have 2 showers and camp free as I arrived late and left early before the collection plate came around. I wouldn't have made it that far if Old Uncle Same didn't love me and continue to send me monthly rations. Beats pushing Bruce another 1000 miles! So Whatever day or night this is, I'm camped in Georgia just south of Chattanooga, Tennessee in the Chattahoochie National Forest in Georgia after riding over 400 miles today. This is also a small section of this forest I was able to stumble upon and camp free as I got trapped in Chattanooga on road detours and no road signs that send you the wrong direction while traffic was heavy. I wrongly thought Chattanooga was a small city so I took the quickest route out I could, having no idea where I was heading. Unfortunately I missed the camp site I was aiming for on Highway 64 to NC before the detours put that out of the question. This will have to do. I'm at a trail head in the forest camped up a hill alone with my Harley below me as Bruce couldn't make it up here. Tomorrow will be some 400 more miles to Ginnie Springs. Hope the weather holds. So far, so good. I'm soon passing 17,000 miles and 2 ½ months on this epic journey!

11/12/17

I'm only now, 2 ½ months later finishing my journal of what I can remember of my last 2 days home to Ormond Beach, FL. I was awakened early at my camp on the Trail head in the Chattahoochie National Forest by dozens of teenage boys and girls preparing to run the trail head to the top of the mountain along with their coaches running right by my tent. That squad of teenage alarm clocks motivated me to finish my final push home, earlier than I planned, being still quite tired. The day was beautiful and once underway, I was supercharged and smelling the finish line, so I ended up riding over 500 miles, my longest distance of any day on my journey to arrive at Gennie Springs campground after dark and just in time to party and celebrate with many of the University of Florida, college students camping there. The place was packed and a band was playing nearby and it didn't take long for people to notice the wild looking bearded man driving up on the Harley looking like Jeremiah Johnson, straight out of the Alaskan wilderness, with my long beard and heavy leathers and camping gear on my Harley, in the middle of August, just north of Gainesville, Fl., surrounded by college kids in swimsuits. Before I knew it, I was the center of attention and the Swamp Hippie band was calling me out on stage to tell my story as we all danced and partied to the music. The band players and other people kept giving me all sorts of gifts, including much whiskey and weed and plenty of food. The next day I kept running into people I didn't remember the night before who remembered me and kept saying "Hello" to Journeyman Joe. This was August 21st 2017, 77 days after I left Florida with Jay and Patty and with whom I parted company in Kansas to continue the journey on my own. It was Jay and Patty who rode over to Ginnie Springs on this day to greet me and welcome me home from my journey we started together. It was both awesome to see them and to know that they are the best kind of friends to have. The kind who don't hold grudges and are happy for you and your accomplishments. My family and I first met Jay and Patty in 1989 when I took an assignment to American Samoa as an Air Traffic Control Specialist, a career from which I'm retired and it turned out we were the only couples on Samoa who had Harleys sent to the island. That was our bond that started our friendship which endures to this day. They are the true veterans of motorcyclying as they have each ridden hundreds of thousands of miles on their bikes. They met me as a rookie who was only a weekend warrior on a bike, but who now has become Journeyman Joe. After we enjoyed partial day at ginnie Springs, I rode the short distance of a few hours home to my awesome wife and kids who supported my journey the whole way and who I could not have completed it withough them enthusiastically cheering me on. As a sidenote, when I returned home, soon thereafter, Florida was hit with much bad weather, including hurricane Irma we had to evacuate from with all our animals and much work to catch up on that delayed this last entry to this journal. Total miles traveled 17, 520 @ 77 days!